Let's find
out about...

CARING FOR
OUR BODIES

Studio Manager: Sara Greasley
Editor: Belinda Weber
Designer: Trudi Webb
Production Controller: Ed Green
Production Manager: Suzy Kelly

ISBN-13: 978-1-84898-084-6 pbk

Copyright © ticktock Entertainment Ltd 2010
First published in Great Britain in 2010 by ticktock Media Ltd,
The Old Sawmill, 103 Goods Station Road, Tunbridge Wells, Kent, TN1 2DP

Printed in China
9 8 7 6 5 4 3 2 1

Picture credits (t=top; b=bottom; c=centre; l=left; r=right; OFC=outside front cover; OBC=outside back cover):
Shutterstock: OFCtr, OFCbr, 4–5 all, 6–7 all, 8–9 all, 11b, 12r, 13 all, 14, 15t, 16–17 all, 19, 20 both, 21b, 22–23 all,
OBC. iStock: OFCbl, 1, 10, 11t, 12l, 15b, 18 both, 21t. Hayley Terry: OFCtl and throughout.

Every effort has been made to trace copyright holders, and we apologize in advance for any omissions.
We would be pleased to insert the appropriate acknowledgments in any subsequent edition of this publication.

Contents

A healthy body

Your body is amazing, but you must look after it to help it stay that way. Eat good food and drink plenty of water, taking lots of **exercise** and rest.

It is important to keep yourself clean. Take baths or showers, wash your hair, and remember to brush your teeth every day.

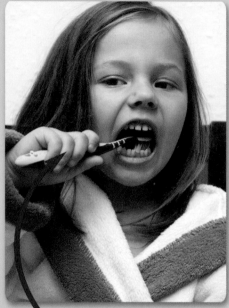

Brush your teeth

What do you like to eat?

You need to eat the right kind of food to be fit and well. Don't eat too much, or too little, as this could make you ill.

Good food gives you **energy** and helps your body grow. Eat lots of fruit and vegetables.

If you don't get enough sleep, you will feel tired and moody the next day.

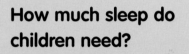

How much sleep do children need?

If you're going to school each day, you'll need about 10 hours of sleep each night. This means you'll be able to pay attention in lessons and learn well.

Exercise helps keep your body strong and healthy.

Eating well

Every day, your body is growing, fighting germs and mending itself. You need to eat healthy food to help your body to do these things.

Fruit and vegetables are full of **vitamins** and **minerals**. Meat, fish, cheese and nuts contain **protein**. All these important nutrients help you stay well.

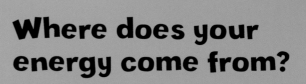

Where does your energy come from?

Your body uses up energy, and you get energy from the food you eat. Taking exercise makes you hungry, because your body needs to replace the energy it has lost.

Why do you get thirsty?

When you feel thirsty, your body is telling you that you need to drink. Your body needs plenty of water to keep working properly. If you don't drink enough, you may feel unwell.

Try to drink about two litres of water a day. That's about eight glasses.

WORD WIZARD!
nutrient
A natural substance in food, that helps to keep you fit and well

How do I keep fit?

A good way to stay healthy is to take plenty of exercise. There are many different kinds of exercise you can do.

Basketball

What's the big deal?

Playing sport makes your **muscles** stronger. It is also good for your bones and **joints**.

Being part of a sports team can be fun. It makes you happy, and it keeps you fit, too.

It is important to be safe when you take exercise. If you ride a bike, always wear a helmet.

Run as fast as you can!

When you run, your heart and lungs work harder than usual. You breathe in fresh air, which is good for you.

What's the problem?

If you don't take any exercise, and eat too much of the wrong kind of food, you will become overweight. This will lead to health problems when you are older.

Burger

TaLKing PoinT

How much exercise do people need?

You should try to get 60 minutes worth of exercise every day. This can be running around, walking to school, or playing games. Just make sure that you're moving!

Burgers are a tasty treat but are a type of junk food. Don't eat them every day.

Heart and lungs

Your heart and lungs both do very important jobs. When you breathe in air, your lungs fill up with oxygen, which goes into your blood. Your heart pumps blood to every part of your body, so it can work properly.

How fit are you?

Running is a good way of making your heart and lungs work extra hard, keeping them fit and healthy.

When you exercise, your heart pumps blood around your body at a faster rate than normal. Your **heartbeat** speeds up.

WORD WIZARD!
polluted
If something is polluted, it is dirty and full of harmful chemicals

Swimming is fun and is good exercise.

What's in the air?

Air contains a gas called oxygen, which you need to stay alive. To keep your lungs healthy, stay away from smoky or polluted places. If somebody in your family smokes, ask them not to smoke near you, so you don't have to breathe smoky air.

Talking Point

What happens to your heart when you run?

Your heart is a muscle and it needs exercise to keep it working properly. When you run, it has to work harder to pump more blood around your body. This helps keep it strong.

Cigarettes are bad for your lungs and heart.

Skin, bones and muscles

Your **skeleton** is made up of 206 bones, which hold your body together and help you stand up straight. Your skin stretches over your body, covering and protecting your bones and muscles.

Muscles pull on your bones to make them move. Exercise keeps your bones and muscles strong.

Skeleton

Do you like sunbathing?

The Sun's rays can be harmful, so protect your skin. Too much sun will burn your skin, making it sore.

Use suncream to protect your skin.

You may break a bone if you have an accident. **X-ray** photographs show where bones are broken.

X-ray of a broken leg

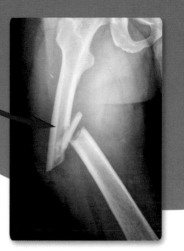

Talking Point

How can you look after your bones?

That's easy! Take lots of exercise, like running and jumping to keep bones strong. Have lots of calcium in your diet to help them grow. And wear protective clothing when you play sport.

What is good for bones?

Eat the right food to keep your bones healthy. Minerals in foods like milk, nuts and fish are good for bones.

Milk and dairy foods contain a mineral called calcium.

Eyes and ears

You have only got one pair of eyes and ears, and they must last your whole life long! Look after them, and remember how important they are.

Your **senses** of sight and hearing help you enjoy the world around you.

Binoculars

Binoculars let you see things that are very far away. They have special lenses that make the thing you're looking at seem much closer than it really is.

WORD WIZARD!
optician
An optician is trained to test your eyesight and provide glasses if you need them

How well can you see?

Many people need to wear glasses to help them see. Visit an optician at least once a year to get your eyesight checked.

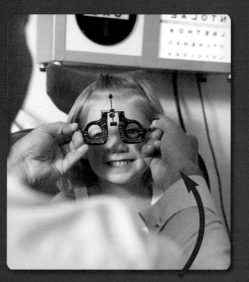

Optician

Is it too loud?

Loud noises can damage your hearing. Turn music down if it is too loud, or wear ear plugs to protect your ears.

Talking point

What are contact lenses?

Contact lenses work like glasses to help people see more clearly. They are tiny lenses that sit on the surface of the eye. Some people prefer to wear contact lenses instead of glasses.

Go to the doctors if you have earache. You may have an ear infection, which will get better with the right medicine.

Why do we have teeth?

You need teeth to bite and chew your food. Your teeth also give you a nice smile! To look after your teeth, brush them every morning and evening, and eat healthy food.

Your first teeth are called your milk teeth. When they fall out, new, bigger ones grow in their place.

Milk teeth

Why bother to brush?

Brushing your teeth gets rid of small bits of food that are stuck on your teeth. This keeps your mouth clean and stops you getting **tooth decay**.

What do dentists do?

Dentists check your teeth and help you look after them. Visit your dentist twice a year for a check-up.

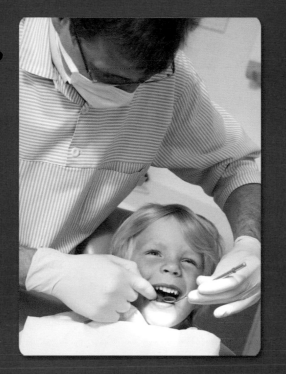

Don't eat too many sugary snacks, because they are bad for your teeth. Always clean your teeth very carefully after you have eaten sweets.

Sugary lolly

Talking Point

When do people grow adult teeth?

By the time you're 14, you'll have 28 adult teeth. Some people grow four more at the back of their mouth when they are about 20 years old. These grinding teeth are called wisdom teeth.

Why are my front teeth so big?

Your front teeth are so big because you use them to bite into your food and chop it up. They are sharper than your back teeth, which you use for grinding your food.

17

Keeping clean

You need to wash yourself every day to keep your body clean. Your skin, nails and hair can get dirty, and if they are not kept clean, they may also begin to smell.

Shampoo

Does that hurt?

If you get a cut or graze on your skin, it is important to wash it carefully and keep it clean. A plaster will stop germs from getting into the cut and causing an **infection**.

Plaster

Dirt contains germs which can make you ill. It is better to stay clean!

Cuts heal more quickly if they are kept clean and dry.

Did you wash your hands?

Don't forget to wash your hands after you have been to the toilet, and before you cook or help in the kitchen. This will stop you from spreading germs to other people.

Use soap when you wash your hands to make sure they are really clean.

Talking Point

Why do people have to wash their hair?

Your hair traps tiny bits of dirt and dust that are in the air. Dirt can contain germs, so washing it away helps keep you germ-free.

WORD WIZARD!
germs
Germs are tiny living things that spread illness. They are so small, you can't see them

19

How can I stay well?

You feel well most of the time, so try to stay that way. Do things that make you happy, like playing with your friends, because this will help you to keep healthy.

Are you feeling ill?

Doctors help you when you are ill. They may tell you to rest, or give you medicine to make you better. They may send you to hospital for special **treatment**.

Having fun and being happy is good for your health.

Never take medicine unless it is given by a doctor, or your parents.

Doctors give people **injections** to protect them from some illnesses.

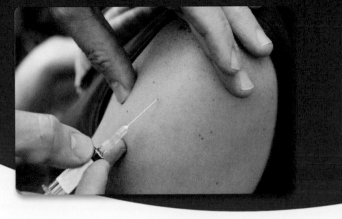

A doctor giving an injection to a patient.

Do you need a hanky?

Always try to use a tissue when you cough or sneeze. This stops you from passing germs on to other people. If you don't have a tissue, sneeze into your sleeve (at the elbow) rather than into your hands.

Talking Point

How can you stop yourself from getting ill?

Everyone gets ill at some time, but you can take steps to protect yourself. Try to have a healthy diet, and keep active to stay fit. Your doctor can give you injections to stop you from catching some illnesses.

Your germs fly through the air when you sneeze. Use a hanky to stop them from spreading too far.

21

Why do we sleep?

Your body never stops working, even when you are asleep. Your heart beats, you keep breathing and your brain carries on thinking. But when you sleep, everything slows down, and your body has a chance to rest.

Are you tired?

If you are feeling ill, your body is telling you that you need to stop and rest. Keep warm, and try to sleep. This will help your body to fight germs.

When you are ill, you need to sleep more than usual.

Lots of sleep

Children need more sleep than adults. Their bodies are growing, which uses up lots of energy.

Sleeping child

Talking Point

How do people relax?

People relax in lots of different ways. Doing something you enjoy, such as reading a book, or listening to music are great ways to relax after a busy day.

Child playing in the sand

Is that fun?

Holidays are a good way of having a change and a rest from your daily routine. It is important to relax and play after working hard.

Glossary

Energy: the strength you get from food to make your body work

Exercise: energetic activity that makes your heart beat faster and your lungs work harder

Heartbeat: the regular beat of your heart as it pumps blood around your body

Infection: an illness that can spread to other people, or other parts of your body

Injection: when a medicine is pushed into your body through a hollow needle

Joint: where two bones fit together

Mineral: a kind of element in food that is good for your health

Muscle: a part of your body that makes you move

Protein: a substance in food that helps your body grow and keeps it strong

Senses: sight, hearing, touch, smell and taste

Skeleton: the body's framework, made of bones

Tooth decay: damage to a tooth caused by sweet food

Treatment: help to make your body well again after an illness or injury

Vitamin: a substance in food that you need to grow and stay healthy

X-ray: a special photograph of the bones in your body. Doctors use X-rays to see if bones are damaged or broken

Index